MOST LIKELY TO DIE

ALSO BY HILARY SIDERIS

The Orange Juice Is Over
Georgetown, KY: Finishing Line Press, 2008

Baby
Columbus, OH: Pudding House Press, 2009

Gold & Other Fish
Georgetown, KY: Finishing Line Press, 2011

Sweet Flag
Georgetown, KY: Finishing Line Press, 2013

MOST LIKELY TO DIE

HILARY SIDERIS

☠

POETS WEAR PRADA • Hoboken, New Jersey

Most Likely to Die

Poets Wear Prada
533 Bloomfield Street, Second Floor
Hoboken, New Jersey 07030
http://pwpbooks.blogspot.com

First North American Publication 2014
First Mass Market Paperback Edition 2014

Grateful acknowledgment is made to the following publications where some of these poems first appeared:

Acoustic Levitation; Amarillo Bay; Avalon Literary Review; Crack the Spine; Forge; Fourteen Hills; Houseboat; The Innisfree Poetry Journal; The Manila Envelope; PoemMemoirStory; Rufous City Review; The Southhampton Review; Spinozablue; Wild Violet; Yes, Poetry.

ISBN-13: 978-0692227695   ISBN-10: 0692227695

Library of Congress Control Number: 2014912259

Printed in the U.S.A.

Front Cover: Roxanne Hoffman

Author Photo: Roxanne Hoffman

For the "Human Riff"

and for my brother, Peter,
whose incessant playing of the Rolling Stones
got me hooked.

"... and I won't forget to put roses on your grave."

-- Mick Jagger & Keith Richards, "Dead Flowers," *Sticky Fingers*, Rolling Stones, April 1971, track 9

Table of Contents

MOST LIKELY TO DIE

▶

ONE

I

MY BLUFF

I built up speed on
Temple Hill, breathed

in heather & gorse,
flew my bike over glory

bumps, into craters
dug by Satan's bombs

on London's burnt
periphery, a puny yokel

with a monkey face,
outpedaling Huns.

DARTFORD

I remember lying in the grass
of our backyard, my mother

pointing at the sky, saying
"Spitfire." The war was over,

but our street ended in blue
horizon, wildflowers, rubble.

A siren sounding still
makes my neck hair curl.

Dartford was full of thieves,
located as it is on Watling,

the old Roman road, atop a steep
hill where the horses stalled,

the perfect spot for a stick-up or toll.
When I grew up,

something was always falling
off a lorry. Someone's wife or

mum showed up in diamonds,
no one asked where from.

BERT

Bert was a printer, a father
with a skill. They bought a tandem,

he & Mum, before the war.
I see them riding through air raids

with me, in the baby seat, puking
from too much sun. Bert never

minded Jesus Christ, nor said there
was no God. He'd see a bloke in

a black frock & cross the road,
that's all. Sometimes, we'd kick

a football on the heath or work
our garden plot. He knew the land:

"Got to get these spuds
in quick." I won't say we were

close. Don't blame him -- Bert
was a fucking working man.

VIOLINS

Grandad Gus wrapped
World War I in gauze,

said he'd been a sniper,
but Bert said Gus never saw

the front. I never heard him
wheeze, but Gus did pawn his

saxophone, saying he had no
wind. It hurt to fiddle --

shrapnel in his palm.
In one story, Gus got gassed

at the Somme. Bert clarified:
"He was a cook. He got

gassed by his own oven."
Gus took me to the violins,

placed me on a high shelf
with a biscuit, cup of tea,

let me watch the bubbling vats,
the men in long brown coats

stirring the glue, twisting
& tempering catgut.

JOANNA

Big-haired, bangled, lighting
Dunhills with a silver Zippo,

she exhaled glamour in our
semidetached house, as if

the Ronettes had arrived.
She made us speculate about

our gypsy blood, all of us
hotheads, harmonizing on

Mum's side. I remember
"When Will I Be Loved"

with Aunt Joanna. She was
a true Dupree. Whatever

crap or masterpiece came
on the radio, we'd try.

13

The best thing that happened
to me (after they dumped me

from Boys' Choir when my
voice broke) was being a Scout,

learning to tie those knots --
the bowline, the sheepshank.

I read all Baden-Powell's manuals:
how to pluck a fowl, gut a squirrel,

ignite a fire with dry twigs
& a magnifier. It gave a boy

a chance to swagger, badges
on his sash, knife in his belt.

I got promoted to squad leader
& I say this in earnest: I kept

my men together & on task.
Years later in our Saint Petersburg

suite, I watched the hundredth
anniversary on TV. The Stones

owe plenty to the Scouts. I stood
& gave the 3-fingered salute:

"Beaver Patrol Leader Richards,
Seventh Dartford, Sir."

SIDCUP ART SCHOOL

Flash sons of bitches
in bow ties, that's what they

tried to turn us into: "Go forth
& advertise." At Sidcup I was

Ricky. No uniforms, no war
to get killed in, we smoked,

grew our hair long, studied
lithography, the light spectrum --

all thrown away on illustrating
Gilbey's gin. We crooned "Cocaine"

in the boys' john. Wizz Jones
dropped by, looking like Jesus,

played South Carolina style,
his fingerpicking taken

from the Reverend Gary
Davis, in Harlem.

DEAR AUNT PAT

Sorry I haven't written. I plead insanity.
I've been so bloody busy since Christmas.

You know I love Chuck Berry. I believed
I was his only English fan until a boy

from my old school comes up to me
in Dartford Station, who's got every 45

Chuck's ever made, plus Howlin' Wolf,
Jimmy Reed -- low-down Chicago stuff;

Bo Diddley, he's another great. Anyways,
the boy's Mick Jagger, & the chicks

& chaps all meet at this juke joint Saturday
night. It's called the Carousel, & Mick's

the world's best R&B singer outside the USA.
We got us a bass player & drummer, too.

Mick lives in a massive, detached house
with a butler who, when I go there, says,

"What can I get you, sir?" So hope all's
well & this explains what's taken me

so long. Luff, Keef (who else would
write this rubbish?)

LEARNING THE BLUES

I wondered for years
how Jimmy Reed played

the 5-chord in the key of E,
not even bothering with B,

the sloppiest possible way --
a great invention. A white guy

in his band taught me & it was
like, that's it? Blues don't go

straight. There's something
wrong, mixed up, flicked

back, suspended like a boy
from school, no rules. It's dark

down here. You feel your way
around. Think of the tune

as something that should
be played by another

instrument, another man,
a horn line, a field hand.

DUST MY BROOM

We trawled the record shops
of Bexleyheath, Mick & me,

among aficionados, horn-rimmed
blokes opposed to amplifiers.

We got a Grundig reel-to-reel
copy of "Diggin' My Potatoes," "Down

the Road Apiece" & "Dust My Broom."
Blokes met in little clumps like

early Christians, muttered matrix
numbers, checked for the shellac

on first printings, guys who
booed Muddy from the back

row when he brought his band
to London, electrified.

DRUMMED

Now Watts, he's the bed I lie on --
musically. Deep down,

he's a jazzman, a condition
I once took it on myself

to rectify. "Charlie swings nicely
but can't rock," I noted in my

teenage diary. "Fabulous guy."
No white man grooves like

Charlie, that illusion of looseness,
sticks through his fingers,

showman-like but no show-off.
When he came on, I'd catch him

humming Parker, Hawkins,
Lester Young. "Cut that shit out.

Listen to fuckin' Muddy. Learn
the blues." I wouldn't even

let him put on Armstrong,
and I love Armstrong.

ERNIES

In my fake leather notebook
I recognize the smudged names

of our gods: Chuck, Muddy, Diddley,
Reed. Five fuck-ups in a Chelsea

flat of dirty plates, we counted
Ernies everywhere we turned.

In every cafe, Ernies perused
menus. "OH CHRIST," we'd say,

"ANOTHER FUCKIN' ERNIE." Only one
thing on *his* mind -- earning

another shilling. Someday
they'd know us not as riffraff,

but blood brothers, lucky sons
born at the midnight hour,

backdoor men. "Mojo working
but" not *just yet* "on you."

MICK

I worked one summer
loading burlap sacks

that cut each time you
slung them over

your shoulder. Sugar's
a motherfucker, but butter --

that nice little square?
I had to hack it from

a boulder while Mick
studied economics.

Spit wads graced our
Edith Grove flat's walls.

He had it harder,
having higher class folks.

We gave them names
like "Goldilocks," "Queen

Green." We had fun.
Mick has changed.

TWO

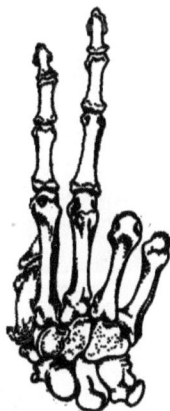

2

CHESS

2120 South Michigan,
the holy house of Chess,

the shrine where every song
we loved was cut -- Willie Dixon,

Chuck Berry, Buddy Guy.
And who's the bloke painting

the place, up on a ladder, whitewash
on his face? Muddy Waters.

Marshall Chess denies this:
"We never had Muddy painting."

But Bill Wyman was there.
He's a witness. Muddy, who

taught us all we knew, lugging
our amps, mopping the studio.

ALL GOD'S DANGERS

They rigged chicken wire
between us & the boys hurling

bottles as their girlfriends raved --
Kentucky, Arkansas, Ohio.

Janitors cleaning up after, winking,
"Good job, fellas, not a dry seat

in the house." Damn bobby-soxers
pissed me off -- hard as the band

had worked to be bluesmen --
they were dying for something,

coming uncorked when Mick
sang Muddy's "Mannish Boy."

We schooled them to their own
country. I'll never forget

the fear of being torn to pieces
by fourteen-year-old girls.

THE LAST TIME

Brian played lead, Vox
white teardrop & Fender

amp, the *wall-of-sound*.
Our first song with

a signature Stones riff.
It goes back to the dawn

of time. Lucky for us,
we stole the chorus

from the Staple Singers,
gave the verse a Teddy

boy twist. Sonny Bono
(before Cher), working for

Phil Spector, drove our
limo to the Biltmore.

1975 WORLD TOUR

I'm told I was driving
a yellow El Camino -- cockpit

stocked with pure Merck coke --
across state lines. Mick got

a tad carried away, inflated cock
emblazoned with the stars

& stripes as he sang "star fucker,
star," a felony in Arkansas.

But Mick's the one who put
a suit on, charmed the Fordyce

mayor & 4-Dice proprietor,
in whose car park I doffed

my cap, "Good morning,
Officers. Oh, was I driving

on the wrong side? Beg your
pardon, I'm English." Then I'm

in handcuffs, with a crowd
outside the courthouse chanting,

"ROCK & ROLL. FREE KEITH."
The judge sipped bourbon

from a hip flask in his sock,
knocked down felonies to mis-

demeanours, & kept my Smith
& Wesson as a souvenir.

ALTAMONT

"High mountain" meant
a field of muddy Harleys

where we played for free,
Hell's Angels as security.

We played for love-hate
& communal anarchy.

You hear it all on *Gimme
Shelter*, the black heart

of human nature, mixed
with rotgut Thunderbird

& bad acid. Was there such
a thing as Flower Power?

We caught a whiff of it,
a headwind from the Haight.

But that night as the dark
came on, we sang in terror,

stage lights in our eyes.
You can't see shit.

I had a knife on me,
and no idea how to use it.

ACID

Pre-Raphaelites in ruffles
searched for the Holy Grail,

the Lost Chord, UFOs. I saw
a flock of yellow birds (really

a willow blowing in the wind),
& I remember how each bird,

as it took flight, gave me
the eye, as if to say, "Try *this*,

it's *so* easy." To trip, you needed
the right friend. With Brian, you

never knew. You'd belly laugh
for hours or march down a dark

sentence, ending in his black dot.
You had to fight to get back to

the crossroads, find the willow,
watch that flock take off again.

PALLENBERG

Only in recklessness
could Brian rival her,

ingesting fistfuls
of downers. Taller

than him, blonder,
polyglottal goddess

of La Dolce Vita Rome,
she was a woman

who could wait -- sit
tight, light up, watch

Brian implode. He beat
his girls, but bouts

with Pallenberg left
his peaches & cream

cheeks purple-green,
his paisley torn,

as she emerged un-
scathed, scathing.

FLASH

"Jack" is "Satisfaction"
in reverse, but if I had

to choose only one riff
to play again, I'd pick

"It's all-l-l right now ..."
I love that hallelujah,

like a chant in Arabic,
almost Gregorian, but

steady-as-you-get-it
rock. The lyric came

at dawn, the unrelenting
Redlands rain, a pair

of spattered Wellies
at the cellar door, Mick

woken by the trudge
& shovel of Jack Dyer,

my Sussex gardener,
starting his day's work.

MARRAKECH

Brian dragged two
tattooed whores --

"hairy whores," Anita
noted -- to their suite.

He pelted her with
room-service food,

then she moved in
with me. I have no

memory of writing
"Brown Sugar" (& my

hat's off if that riff's
Mick's) but I recall

Cecil Beaton drinking
a toast to our torsos.

SPEEDBALLS

"Let me be clear about this. I don't have a drug problem. I have a police problem."
-- Keith Richards

A little Tuinal at tea time
or for breakfast on the road

helped with the lack of jam
& scones. I played for days

on downers, not for pleasure,
but to shift from shitty fame

to busy lull, till I discovered
speedballs: cocaine & heroin

to take you up, bring you back
down. I still can't fathom

why Scotland Yard bothered
to tap our phones, plant acid

in our cars? Chasing a band
of tripping troubadours,

how fucking bored
were those coppers?

THREE

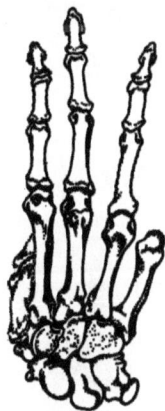

3

LENNON

John Winston Lennon, 1940-1980

A silly sod in many ways,
John was. I liked to tease

him for the way he wore
his Fender high, under his

chin. "Try a longer strap,
John, FOR CHRIST'S SAKE.

It's not a violin. No wonder
you lugs only rock,

can't roll." But they thought
it was cool. Maybe you

had to be from Liverpool.
He wasn't one to mince

opinions, said my solo
on "It's All Over Now"

reeked, & he was right.
He was my mate.

GRAM

Cecil Ingram Connor III (aka Gram Parsons),
1946-1973

I needed a cure before
the US tour, & so did he,

before his wedding day.
There's Parsons -- *the only*

guy ever -- & me,
in my 4-poster bed. We're

wild with pain, can't stop
twitching: "OH, GOD,

HERE COMES SMITTY,"
our sadistic Cornish nurse,

the dominatrix of *aversion*
therapy, injecting saline

& disgrace: "Stop sniveling,
mate. You wouldn't be here

if you weren't a cunt." Bill
Burroughs swore by her.

PRESTON
William Everett "Billy" Preston, 1946-2006

I took him backstage, flashed
a blade, You're gonna feel this,

Bill, if you don't turn your organ
down. This ain't the Billy Preston

band. You are the keyboard
player for the Rolling Stones.

He was one fucked-up virtuoso,
gay before you could be, child

of the church choir, with a wide
mean streak. Completely bald.

Once I pulled him off his boyfriend
on an elevator in Innsbruck --

HE WAS PUMMELING THE BLOKE.
Then I bent down,

scooped it off the floor,
that ludicrous Afro he wore.

RINGING A BELL

Johnnie Johnson, 1924-2005

Chuck played piano keys,
A-flat, E-flat, on his Gibson.

It was the Sir John Trio when
Chuck came along to sign

the contracts, do the math.
But Johnnie -- *couldn't "B.*

Goode" -- showed up shitfaced,
refused to board the plane.

He was driving a bus
in St. Louis, tiredest man

I've ever had the honor
to work with -- "bus driver" tired.

He held no grudge.
He played the tunes,

he said, but it took Chuck
to write them down.

CHUCK'S BLUES

"Leave the amp as I set it. That's my amp and I'm setting it the way I wish it ... That's the way Chuck Berry plays it, you understand? ... I've been living for 60 years with it."

-- *Chuck Berry*

Each line in rhythm
& blues embellishes

that one idea: The boss
man's mean; You hurt

me bad; You talk
too much; I'm nothing

without you. What Chuck did
for white America was

sing it straight & clean:
"Oh Daddy, Daddy,

may I go?" begs "Sweet
Little 16." "Whisper to

Mommy, it's all right
with you." Then "back in

class again." He was
one angry man.

HAIL HAIL

"The teacher is teachin' the Golden Rule ..."
-- Chuck Berry, "School Day (RING RING
Goes the Bell)," Chess, March 1957

Something about the total
brilliant sound. It flew

off the needle the first time
I put his record on.

It made me love the man,
let me put up with him in years

to come -- the only bastard
I didn't punch back.

I was just proud not to go down.
He'd sidle over mid solo,

the son of a bitch, whisper
in my ear, "After this chorus,

let's switch to B-flat, shake it up,
give Keef a problem to work out."

Nothing malicious, just
Chuck being Chuck.

FOUR

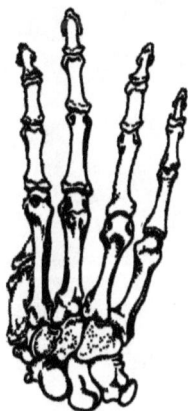

4

HYDRAULIC FAULT

I flipped her over, & Anita broke
her collarbone. At Saint Richard's

they patched us up. Thank God for
brilliant doctors doing their work.

3 in the fucking morning, &
they're everywhere -- bad-mannered

cops & cameramen. I wasn't even
using at the time. A red light on

the dashboard flashed, the brakes
& steering locked, but the amazing

windscreen held with three tons
rolling on her. My '47 Mercedes:

Panzer scrap & Fuhrer steel.
No wonder France fell in six weeks.

PALLENBERG UNBOUND

"Ice Queen," they called her,
"Rude Girl," "Mussolini" for

the way she rolled her Rs.
I was on tour. She fractured

a sergeant's skull, shattered
his Ray-Bans, dumping the works

from the top storey of our villa
Point of View. They threw her

in a Steer Town cell,
tossed her a blanket, a bucket.

Now what the hell were they
to do but drop the charges,

make her swear never again to
shipwreck on Jamaican shores? --

fuckin' shame 'cause I could've
put down roots among

the Rastafarians, who called
me "Our Man Up North."

EXILE

It's hard today to understand
why we recorded our best album

in the basement of my house
at Cap Ferrat, built by an English

banker who got sick of British
tax & shabbiness. A staircase

led to a grotto & my speedboat
Mandrax. No navigation needed:

skirt the coastline to Marseilles --
smugglers, sailors, & palaces

of whores. Anita wouldn't board,
said I knew nothing about sub-

merged rocks. But I soon learned.
For a boat, the danger's land.

HIS DEMISE

Lewis Brian Hopkins Jones, 1942-1969

It could have been mine,
the papers opined --

as usual, wrong, because
that death belonged

to Brian -- an unwell lad,
often unkind, who loved

no one & nothing but
the blues, weak lunged,

thin skinned. I come from
sturdier stock. I always

figured I'd live long.
Look at Gram.

FIRSTBORN

Switzerland, Austria,
Germany, boom, "You'd

better wake up, Dad." Time
to pull over, take your shot,

& toss that shit. Marlon knew
the ins & outs, each country's

capital & flag, the checkpoint
soldiers' uniforms. What can

a father do? Mum's a junkie.
Dad's on permanent tour.

I gave him a job, paid him
in ice cream cones. My boy

of seven -- pure enthusiasm,
able to read a map.

TARA

One night as we were going onstage,
I got the "I'm-so-sorry-to-tell-you" call.

What happened only Anita knows.
I think I changed his nappy twice.

Crib Death. We never spoke of it.
Every lovely one of us should leave

this world, all in the natural order,
dad, mum. But seeing a baby off?

You just go numb. Only years later
do the waves of love, visions of who

he was or would've been wash
over you. He'll never let me go.

MOST LIKELY TO DIE

The necromantic press
crowned me "Prince

of Darkness," world's most
wasted wealthy lad. First

you're a novelty, a fad.
You'll fade like rock & roll,

they reckon. Then you don't.
You piss 'em off. They write

a most-likely-to-die list,
make you number one.

Rumors abound: "He flies
to Zurich to change his blood."

You lose some teeth,
the death mask fits.

Ten years I topped that chart.
It almost hurt to fall to fifth.

My fans still send me
skulls by the truckload.

SMACK

Robert Louis Balfour Stevenson, 1850-1894

"I thought of Keith because I was trying to figure out what pirates might have been like ... I thought, oh man, they were the rock and roll stars of the era. ... And ... the greatest rock and roll star of all time ... Keith Richards hands down."
— *Johnny Depp,* Blunt Review, *2003*

Well, I could lecture you
on quality -- or could've --

now my tips are obsolete.
I could implore you never to try,

trade in an outlaw's pride
in being bad for a knighthood.

I'll say what Billy Bones said, begging
a child, against the doctor's orders,

to bring rum: What does a doctor know
about seafaring men, who've been

in places hot as tar, the terra firma
heaving like the sea, & mates

dropping all 'round from yellow jack
or hanged & drying in the sun?

What does he know
of lands like that?

MUSH MOUTH

Mathis James "Jimmy" Reed, 1925-1976

I'm told there's a Jimmy
Reed church & I believe

the soul craves catchy tunes,
two-string turnarounds.

So what if he stumbled
onstage, mumbled the words?

Why stress about his ungreatness,
the way he stripped laconic

down to slur? Chess never got it --
that's their loss -- his lack,

his slacker's lope that gave us
hope to jelly roll.

Sometimes the boss man
ain't that big, just tall.

THE DRONE

The moment you tune
your guitar to one chord,

you have to learn where not
to put your fingers, what to

leave alone. Imagine a piano
turned upside down, the white

keys black, an ocean pulsing
in a shell. African tribesmen,

Vivaldi, Mozart knew
you let one note jangle

& throb behind the brain.
The same train takes you

from the Delta to Detroit --
the human heartbeat.

CALLED

It doesn't come to you.
You go to fame.

You don't negotiate,
you nod your head, stick

to the road you're on.
Sometimes you'd like to exit,

but you're dazzled,
stupefied, & under contract

to provide. The great ones --
Muddy, Robert Johnson --

sold their solid-duty souls.
Why would the likes

of us not follow them
to the crossroads?

Acknowledgments

We extend our thanks to the editors of the following publications where several of these poems first appeared:

Acoustic Levitation

"Joanna" (as "1954"),
"1975 World Tour,"
"Altamont,"
"All God's Dangers,"
"Chess," "Marrakech,"
"Mick,"
"Dust My Broom" (as
  "Sweep My Broom")

Amarillo Bay

"Called"

Avalon Literary Review

"Hydraulic Fault"

Crack the Spine

"HAIL HAIL,"
"Mush Mouth"

Forge

"Smack," "Speedballs,"
"The Last Time"

Fourteen Hills

"The Violins"

Houseboat

"Exile," "Firstborn,"
"Pallenberg Unbound,"
"Most Likely to Die" (as
  "Skulls"),
"Tara"

The Innisfree Poetry Journal

"The Drone"

The Manila Envelope

"Pallenberg,"
"Dear Aunt Pat"

PoemMemoirStory	"My Bluff"
Rufous City Review	"Learning the Blues" (as "Keith's Blues")
The Southhampton Review	"Chuck's Blues" (as "Chuck"), "His Demise"
Spinozablue	"Bert," "Ernies," "Flash," "Sidcup Art School," "13" (as "Thirteen")
Wild Violet	"Lennon"
Yes, Poetry	"Dartford," "Drummed," "Acid"

About the Author

Hilary Sideris is the author of four poetry chapbooks: *The Orange Juice Is Over* (Finishing Line Press, 2008), *Baby* (Pudding House Press, 2009), *Gold & Other Fish* (Finishing Line Press, 2011), and *Sweet Flag* (Finishing Line Press, 2013). Her work appears in the anthologies *Pomegranate Seeds: An Anthology of Greek American Poetry*, edited by Dean Kostos (Somerset Hall Press, 2008); *Token Entry: NYC Subway Poems*, edited by Gerry LaFemina (Smalls Books / Red Lashes Productions, 2012); and in the forthcoming *Rabbit Ears: Poems About TV*, edited by Joel Allegretti. Sideris studied English Literature at Indiana University and attended The University of Iowa Writers' Workshop. She lives in Brooklyn and works for The City University of New York, where she develops and coordinates programs for English language learners and first-generation college students.

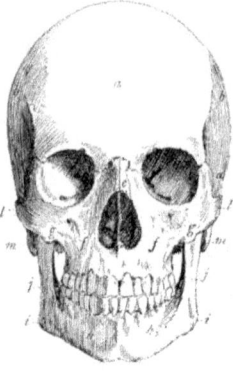

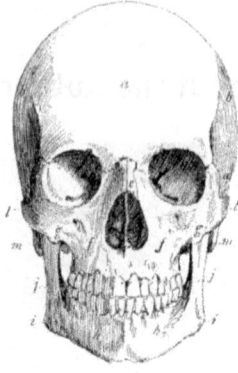

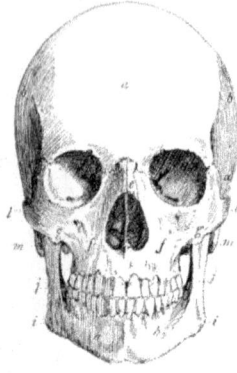

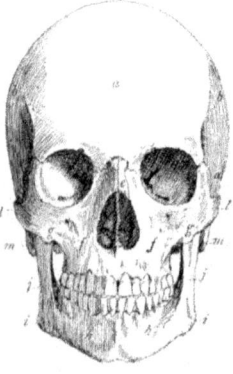

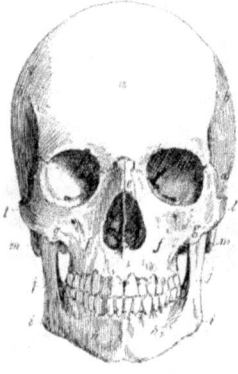

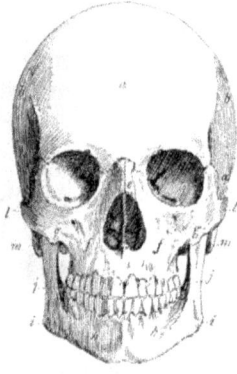

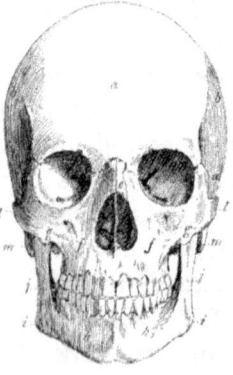

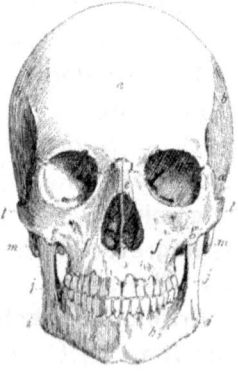

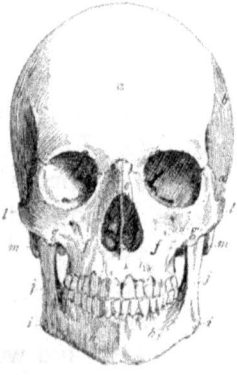

A NOTE ON THE TYPE

The poems in this book are set in Transport Medium, a sans serif typeface designed for British road signs by Jock Kinneir and his assistant Margaret Calvert, between 1957 and 1963, as part of their work as graphic designers for the United Kingdom's Department of Transport, in anticipation of Britain's first motorway, (London - Yorkshire) M1. All manner of signage using Transport Medium and its sister font Transport Heavy was investigated and initially tested on the Preston bypass (1958, now part of the M6 motorway), before their introduction on the M1 motorway a year later. Designed with an eye for legibility at a distance, but with that British flair for style, Kinneir and Calvert developed a rounded typeface with distinctive tails to 'a', 't', and 'l', and bar-less fractions, all of which aided legibility.

To this day the Transport typefaces remain the only ones allowed on United Kingdom road signs (except for motorway signs, where route numbers appear in their own separate typeface known as Motorway, also designed by Kinneir and Calvert).

Before the Worboys Report introduced the current UK road sign designs and lettering in 1964, British road signs looked very different. The title, half title, section title pages of this book are set in a narrower typeface typical of pre-Worboys road signs used around Birmingham, UK. The font, AES Ministry, is by Harry Blackett.